D0753641

DISCARD

Venus _{and} Serena Williams

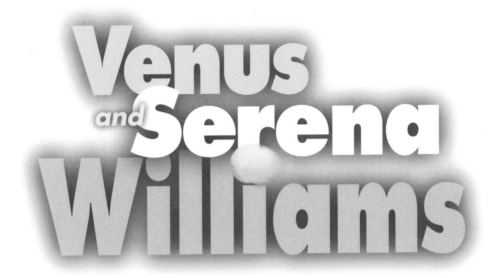

Venus and Serena Williams

grand slam sisters

Terri Morgan

LERNER
SPORTS
AN IMPRINT OF LERNER PUBLISHING GROUP

For my cousin Susan

This book is available in two editions:
Library binding by LernerSports
Soft cover by First Avenue Editions
Imprints of Lerner Publishing Group
241 First Avenue North
Minneapolis, MN 55401 U.S.A.

Website address: www.lernerbooks.com

Library of Congress Cataloging-in-Publication Data

Morgan. Terri,
    Venus and Serena Williams : grand slam sisters / by Terri Morgan.
        p.   cm.
    Includes bibliographical references and index.
    ISBN 0–8225–3684–6 (lib. bdg. : alk. paper)
    ISBN 0–8225–9866–3 (pbk : alk. paper)
    1. Williams, Venus, 1980– Juvenile literature. 2. Williams, Serena, 1981–
Juvenile literature. 3. Tennis players—United States—Biography—Juvenile
literature. 4. African American women tennis players—Biography—Juvenile
literature. [1. Williams, Venus, 1980– 2. Williams, Serena, 1981– 3. Tennis
players. 4. African Americans—Biography. 5. Women—Biography.]
I. Title.
GV994.A1 M67 2001
796.342'092'273—dc21   00–012800

Manufactured in the United States of America
1 2 3 4 5 6 – JR – 06 05 04 03 02 01

Contents

Serena doesn't let the large crowds distract her during the 1999 U.S. Open.

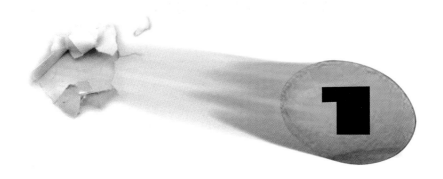

Serena's Grand Slam

On September 11, 1999, Serena Williams was one point away from winning the biggest tennis match of her life—and realizing a long-standing dream. Ever since she first picked up a tennis racket as a four year old and began hitting balls on a cracked court in Compton, California, Serena had dreamed about winning the U.S. Open. On a hot September afternoon in New York, the seventeen year old finally had a chance to make her dream come true. "I was always the one to say 'I want the U.S. Open,'" Serena noted. "Venus [Serena's older sister] always wanted Wimbledon."

Serena's journey from one of California's poorest cities to **center court** at one of the world's most elite tennis tournaments had captivated sports fans everywhere. Even people who had never picked up a racket or followed the game were enthralled with Serena Williams and her sister, Venus. Born just fifteen months apart, the bright and bubbly sisters dazzled fans with their powerful strokes, great speed, and impressive savvy on the court. Their braided and beaded hair and stylish tennis outfits also attracted fans.

As two of the few African Americans on the professional tennis circuit, the sisters were often compared to another groundbreaking young athlete from a minority family. "She's the Tiger Woods of tennis," said Bud Collins, a tennis reporter for NBC television, when Venus started playing professionally. Later, many people made the same comparison about Serena.

Serious tennis fans also took notice, especially when the sisters were invited to play in top-ranked tournaments like the U.S. Open. The open is one of four "grand slam" events on the international tennis circuit. The All-England Lawn Tennis Championships (commonly called Wimbledon), the Australian

Open, and the French Open are the other three. The U.S. Open draws the best players from around the globe, and a victory there can send a player straight to the top of the tennis rankings.

Like most pro tournaments, the U.S. Open is an **elimination tournament.** Players pair off against one another in the first round of competition. Winners advance to the second round to face other first-round winners. With each round, half the field is eliminated, until only two players remain. They compete against one another in the finals for the tournament title.

Few people, except Serena and her family, expected the youngest of the Williams sisters to make it past the early rounds in the 1999 U.S. Open. Going into the tournament, she had played in fewer than two dozen professional events, and many people thought that this lack of experience would hurt her chances. But Serena's father, Richard, scoffed at the naysayers. He boldly predicted that Serena and her sister Venus would face each other in the final round of the elimination tournament. "It will be a Williams-Williams final," he said. When asked who would win, Richard Williams would say only, "A Williams!"

Of the two sisters, Venus had the most experience. Ranked third in the world going into the tournament, she had reached the finals of the event two years earlier. But Switzerland's Martina Hingis had taken the title that year, shattering Venus's dreams of victory. Venus met Hingis again in the 1999 U.S. Open, this time in the semifinal round (one round before the finals).

Venus's powerful serve, clocked at 121 miles per hour, was one of her best weapons. Facing Hingis, however, her control disappeared during the first **set.** Instead of slamming the ball across court, Venus repeatedly drove it into the net. Hingis took advantage of those errors, winning the first set six games to one. (In tennis, the first player to win six games, with a lead of at least two games, wins the set. In women's competition, the first player to win two sets wins the match.)

Venus rallied in the hard-fought second set, besting Hingis 6–4. But, exhausted from the battle, she tired in the decisive third set. With the score tied 3–3, Venus's right leg began cramping. She remained on the court but was unable to hold off her opponent. A disappointed Venus was a good sport after Hingis closed out the third and final set with a score of 6–3.

Venus served up a tough game at the 1999 U.S. Open but was eventually beaten by Martina Hingis.

Serena, on the other hand, was unstoppable in the tournament. After defeating Monica Seles in the quarterfinals (two rounds before the finals), Serena faced defending U.S. Open champion Lindsay Davenport in the semifinals. Taking the first set 6—4, Serena was confident heading into the second set. So was Davenport, who began to play more aggressively. After losing the second set 1—6, Serena rebounded in the third and final set. With the score tied 3—3, Serena relied on her wits and her powerful serve. The combination allowed her to capture the next three games and put her into the championship match.

The final, played at center court, pitted Serena against Martina Hingis. Ranked as the world's number-one female player, Hingis presented a tough challenge. Playing in her third straight U.S. Open final, Hingis remembered that she had lost the 1998 title to Davenport. Hingis was hungry to regain the title—at Serena's expense.

Focused on her lifelong dream, Serena was just as determined. She wanted to win the title and stop Hingis's return to the winner's circle. With her father, her mother, Oracene, and her sister Venus watching from the stands, Serena easily took the first set. In the second set, leading five games to three, Serena

Serena tries her best to stop Martina Hingis from winning the 1999 U.S. Open.

was brimming with confidence. But a point away from the prized U.S. Open title, Serena's play suddenly changed.

The 22,000 fans packed into Arthur Ashe Stadium watched in amazement as her willpower seemed to disappear. Two **unforced errors** allowed Hingis to bring the set to 5–4. With Serena clearly rattled, Hingis evened the set at 5–5, then took the lead.

Serena recovered, briefly, to bring the score to 6–6. This set up a play-off game called a **tiebreaker.**

Realizing she had a second chance to put the match away, Serena talked herself back into the contest. "There comes a time when you just have to stop caving in," Serena said afterward. "I told myself 'whether you win or lose, you're going to have to perform.'"

Her determination restored, Serena took the lead in the tiebreaker. She was up six points to four, but Hingis continued fighting. (In a tiebreaker, the first player to reach seven points, with a lead of at least two points, wins the set.) Then Hingis made a backhand shot that landed just outside the court, giving Serena the winning point and leaving her both shocked and overjoyed. Clutching her chest, then her head, the young champion shouted, "Oh my God, I won," before rushing to the stands to reach her family. "I didn't know what to do, laugh, or cry or scream," Serena told reporters after the match. "So I did it all."

Serena won her second U.S. Open crown the following day. She and her partner—Venus—had reached the finals in women's **doubles tennis.** Facing Chanda Rubin and Sandrine Testud, the Williams sisters dropped the first set. But they came roaring back, winning the next two sets 6—1 and 6—4 to take the match.

The Williams sisters' sweep at the grand slam event sent a powerful message to the sporting world: Tennis's new stars were a double force to be reckoned with.

Serena became the first African-American woman to win the U.S. Open since 1958, when Althea Gibson captured the title.

Richard Williams and his daughter Venus at the tennis courts in Compton, California, 1990

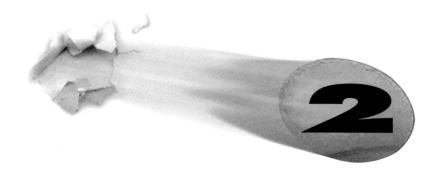

Ghetto Cinderellas

Venus and Serena Williams were destined to become tennis players even before they were born. Their father, Richard Williams, was a gifted athlete who excelled in basketball, football, and golf as a high-school student in Shreveport, Louisiana. But Richard had never been interested in tennis while growing up. In fact, as a teenager, he thought tennis was a "sissy game."

After graduating from high school, he took a job as a construction worker. Eventually, he moved to Southern California and opened a successful security business. Richard married Oracene Price, a nurse, and had three daughters, Yetunde, Isha, and

Lyndrea. He wanted his children to be even more successful than he was when they grew up.

For Richard, the tennis bug began not on the court but on the couch in his living room, while watching tennis on TV. "I saw this person win all this money," Richard told *Newsweek* magazine. So he decided to turn his kids into tennis players.

He first taught himself how to play by watching instructional videos, reading books about tennis, and practicing on public courts. Then he began teaching the game to his three little girls. Yetunde was seven, Isha was six, and Lyndrea was one when their sister Venus Ebone Starr was born on June 17, 1980. Serena was born the next year, on September 26, 1981. Richard made plans to teach his youngest daughters tennis as well.

Venus went with her father, mother, and older sisters to the local tennis courts even before she entered kindergarten. "I was 4½ when I first picked up a racket," Venus told *Seventeen* magazine. "My sisters and I would each take turns hitting with my mom and dad. My entire family played almost every day."

While Yetunde, Isha, and Lyndrea were good players, it was clear from the start that Venus was especially gifted. She fell in love with the game right away. Like her father, she was extremely well coordinated. She was also strong for her age, mentally tough, confident, and sure of herself on the court. "She was a champion the first day," Richard recalled.

The Williams family was living in Compton, California, when Venus started playing tennis. Located near Los Angeles, Compton is home to many low-income African-American and Latino families. Drug use and gang violence are common problems in the area. "AK-47s, drugs . . . and welfare checks are more prevalent [in Compton] than anywhere else in the world," Richard said. The only tennis courts near the family's home were located in gang territory. Richard jokingly nicknamed the cracked, graffiti-covered courts "the East Compton Hills Country Club."

After Serena turned four, she too began playing tennis. Like Venus, she showed a great talent for the sport. To save money, Richard picked up stray tennis balls from nearby courts. He practiced with his two youngest daughters every afternoon, patiently hitting hundreds of balls to them. Along with teaching Venus and Serena how to hit balls over the net, Richard had to teach them how to hit the ground when gunfights broke out between gang members nearby. Eventually, he befriended the gang members in the neighborhood. Impressed by Richard's dedication to his daughters, the gang members agreed to keep the peace while the girls were playing.

Shortly after Venus began playing tennis, Richard realized that she was becoming obsessed by the sport. So he did something many coaches thought was unusual: He said five-year-old Venus couldn't play tennis for a year. Later he explained that he was trying to raise a good human being instead of just a good tennis player. "When someone loves something too much it's more detrimental than a person who doesn't love it at all," Richard said.

The layoff gave Venus more time to play soccer, tag, hopscotch, hide-and-seek, and other games with her sisters. It also made her realize how much she enjoyed playing tennis. So when Richard returned her racket to her, Venus was even more eager to play. She looked forward to the afternoons when she and Serena would go with their father to the "East Compton Hills Country Club." The two would practice for hours, doing drills Richard invented.

School was also important in the Williams family. Richard said that Venus and Serena had to do their homework and keep their grades up if they wanted to play tennis. Both girls liked school and worked hard in the classroom. They frequently brought home report cards with A's in all the subjects.

The Williams sisters began attracting attention when they started playing in junior tennis tournaments. Venus did extremely well. By the time she was ten, she had won seventeen matches in a row to capture the Southern California championship for girls age twelve and under. Respected coaches and professional players raved about Venus's game. "She's headed for Grand Slam titles," longtime tennis coach John Wilkerson told *Sports Illustrated* magazine in 1991.

Sports agents and coaches began calling, asking to work with Venus, whom Richard nicknamed "the Ghetto Cinderella." Newspapers, national magazines, and even television news shows like *60 Minutes* interviewed Venus. The media focus was so great that Venus and Serena had to switch schools three times so they could attend classes undisturbed.

As the older of the two sisters, Venus drew attention away from Serena, who was also winning junior tournaments—forty-six out of forty-nine matches. Richard soon began limiting the number of tournaments his daughters entered. He didn't want them to

Venus and Serena, junior tennis stars, pose with former president Ronald Reagan.

burn out in the ultra-competitive world of junior tennis. When Venus was eleven, Richard had her quit playing the junior circuit entirely. As an undefeated player, with a record of sixty-three wins and zero losses, she had nothing else to prove at the junior level. Richard wanted Venus to focus on her schoolwork instead of her tennis game. "She needs time to get an education," he said. "Because all these girls who come along chewing gum and not being able to speak that well, what happens to them when their careers are over?"

Richard had Serena stop playing in junior tournaments as well. He said that racism on the tennis circuit played a part in his decision. "When a white girl lost to my daughter the parent would say 'You let me down. How could you let that [black girl] beat you?'" he told *Newsweek*. "I didn't want my kids growing up around that."

But Venus and Serena kept practicing. And even though Richard limited their practices to three times a week, they kept getting better and better.

Graffiti, gangs, drugs, and guns threatened Venus's tennis practice in Compton, California.

Venus, left, **and Serena,** right, **soon outgrew their father's excellent but limited coaching ability.**

Champions in Training

Richard Williams planned to coach Venus and Serena as long as they continued playing. A gifted athlete and self-taught tennis player, Richard was confident he could teach them the finer points of the game. But by 1991, Richard realized his budding superstars, especially Venus, understood the game even better than he did. He decided they needed a professional coach if they were going to continue to improve.

For several years, tennis coaches had been eager to work with the girls—especially Venus, the older and taller of the two sisters. Although Richard and Oracene had turned down many offers in the past, they did allow several coaches to watch the girls practice. One of those coaches was Rick Macci, who worked at the International Tennis Academy in Orlando, Florida. When Venus was ten, Macci flew out to California to see her play tennis with Serena.

Macci was used to watching outstanding young players. But when Macci saw Venus play for the first time, his jaw dropped with amazement. She was one of the most gifted athletes he had ever seen. He was even more impressed with Venus's athletic ability when she left the court to visit the bathroom. "As she walks out the gate she walks at least 10 yards on her hands," Macci told a reporter for *Tennis* magazine. "I was stunned. Then she went into these backward cartwheels for another 10 yards. I'm watching this and the first thing I thought was 'I've got a female Michael Jordan on my hands.'"

At that time, tuition at the tennis academy was $2,200 a month. Richard couldn't afford that. But Macci was moving to Fort Lauderdale, Florida, to work at the Inverray Racquet Club. He offered to coach both Venus and Serena there for free. After talking it over, Richard and Oracene decided to accept the offer. Richard felt that Venus and Serena were too young to be separated from the rest of their

The young and talented Venus was called "a female Michael Jordan."

family. So he sold his security business, and Oracene quit her nursing job. Then they packed up everything and moved to southern Florida with all five daughters.

The family settled in a home at Delray Beach, north of Fort Lauderdale. Richard and Oracene enrolled Venus and Serena, then ages eleven and ten, in local public schools. After classes ended for the day, Richard drove the sisters to the club for tennis practice. Playing six hours a day, six days a week, both girls worked very hard to improve their games. Later, Richard and Oracene decided to homeschool their daughters, teaching the girls at the family home. This arrangement gave Venus and Serena more time with the family and fewer outside distractions.

The Williams family was extremely close knit. They were also serious about their religion. Venus and Serena, their sisters, and their mother all belong to a religious group called Jehovah's Witnesses.

Jehovah's Witnesses follow a strict moral code that prohibits smoking, drinking, drug use, and gambling. As athletes, Venus and Serena understood that following this code—especially staying away from cigarettes, alcohol, and drugs—would help them stay healthy.

Their devotion to their religion wasn't the only thing that set Venus and Serena apart from the other young tennis players Macci coached. While the other kids played regularly in junior tournaments,

Rick Macci offered to coach the Williams sisters for free if they moved to Florida.

Richard still wouldn't allow Venus and Serena to compete. He thought that competition would distract them from their studies and the joys of childhood. "I'm not going to let Venus pass up on her childhood," Richard explained. "Long after tennis is over, I want her to know who she is."

Although many people criticized Richard's decision, Coach Macci respected it. "[Richard] had done what he thought in his heart was best for his girls," Macci said. "He gets an A-triple plus for being the type of parent he is. He's got educated, well-mannered kids who have their priorities in line."

Macci also felt that Venus in particular did not need to play in tournaments to hone her skills. "All kids are competitive, but her competitiveness is a couple of levels deeper," Macci told *People* magazine. "She'll run over broken glass to hit a ball."

At age fourteen, three years after she played her last match as a junior, Venus began begging her parents to let her play professionally. The right-handed youngster felt she was ready to compete against the world's best female tennis players. At 6 feet, 1 inch (and still growing), Venus was taller than most of the women on the pro circuit. She knew her height would be an advantage on the court. She could get to—and stretch to—the ball quicker than shorter opponents could. Venus was also confident. "I'm strong, I'm tall, I work hard on the court, and I have the right technique," she told *Seventeen*.

Her parents, however, wanted her to wait. "If I have my way, Venus won't turn pro until she is 18 or 19, maybe 20," Richard Williams said. Oracene also tried to talk Venus into postponing her professional career. But Venus insisted she was ready. Oracene told *Ebony* magazine that Venus "kept bugging" her until Oracene gave Venus permission to play.

That permission came with several conditions. To keep Venus from burning out on competition, Richard told his daughter that she could play in no more than five tournaments each year. Venus agreed, even though she wouldn't get as much tournament experience as other pros, who played in twelve to fourteen events annually. Venus, who by then had switched from homeschooling to private school, also agreed that she would stop competing if her grades dropped. "Education is more important than tennis right now," Venus said. "Whatever I put in my head will stay there forever, but that's not necessarily true of tennis."

Richard Williams asked his daughter to do one more thing before starting as a pro. She planned to launch her professional career in Oakland, California, at the Bank of the West Classic in late October. Before the tournament, Richard wanted her to speak to youngsters living in low-income areas in Oakland, a largely African-American city, and to encourage them to stay in school. Venus agreed willingly. "I know I should go [to the low-income neighborhoods] because that's where I'm from," Venus said.

The "Ghetto Cinderella" did not want to forget her roots—but she also had big plans for the future.

Venus smiles while proving herself at her first professional match in 1994.

Venus in the Spotlight

On October 31, 1994, ten years after Venus first picked up a tennis racket, the big day arrived. Her braided hair strung with 1,800 colorful beads, she walked onto the court for her first professional match, at the Bank of the West Classic in Oakland, California. While the spotlight rarely shines on newcomers to the pro circuit, Venus's debut attracted widespread attention. Thanks to all the publicity she had received over the years, an army of reporters came to watch her play. Photographers followed her movements both on and off the court.

Venus did not disappoint her audience. It took the teenage prodigy just two sets to defeat twenty-five-year-old Shaun Stafford, ranked fifty-ninth in the world. Although she beat Stafford easily, Venus ran into trouble in her second-round match. There she faced the world's number-two player, Arantxa Sanchez-Vicario of Spain. Venus captured the first set, 6–2, but Sanchez-Vicario took the next two sets, 6–3 and 6–0, and won the match.

Although she hadn't gone far in the tournament, Venus captured the hearts of many people when she thanked the crowd for helping make her first pro contest so much fun. When fans approached her after the match, she cheerfully signed autographs. The well-spoken teen also charmed the reporters who interviewed her after the loss. "I like answering questions," Venus said. "I think it's fun."

As well as fun, professional tennis was very profitable. As an amateur player, Venus had refused all offers made by companies that wanted her to endorse (help sell) their products. As a professional, however, she began considering offers, including one from the Reebok company. Reebok sells athletic shoes, clothing, and equipment. The firm offered to pay Venus $3 million a year to use and promote

Venus first signed a Reebok contract in 1995. The company renewed her contract in 2000, agreeing to pay her nearly $40 million over five years.

their products for five years. After carefully considering the deal, Venus and her parents accepted the offer early in 1995.

The money allowed the Williams family to move into a new home. Since Venus was becoming so well known, privacy was very important to the family. They chose a modest brick house surrounded by ten acres of land in Palm Beach Gardens, Florida.

Neither the house nor the tennis court in the backyard could be seen from the street.

The funds also allowed the Williams family to pay training partners—former male tennis pros—to practice with Venus and Serena. Richard had begun coaching his daughters again, and he wanted them to get experience playing against stronger opponents. After finishing classes at their private school at 12:30, Venus and Serena would spend the rest of the afternoon practicing tennis. While they played, Richard and Oracene took turns encouraging them and praising them for good shots. Richard would jokingly remind Venus of her goals when she made a great shot. "Here comes the Wimbledon trophy," Richard said. "Let me hold the purse."

In the evenings, after dinner with the family, the two hit their schoolbooks. Both Serena and Venus embraced their studies with enthusiasm. "Science is my favorite subject," Venus said. "Can you believe that in 1923 explorers found a prehistoric fish off the coast of Madagascar that was supposed to be extinct, like, five hundred million years ago? Learning about that stuff is so cool."

While the limelight shone brightly on Venus, Serena remained partially hidden in the shadows.

Few people except family members, training partners, and her former coach, Rick Macci, paid much attention to her game. Those players who joined her on the court, however, came away impressed. One of them was retired professional Pam Shriver, who once spent several days practicing with Serena and her celebrity sister. "Serena's forehand wasn't big on control, but as far as power . . . wow!" Shriver said. "She was just cracking the ball."

The fact that one of the top female players was impressed with her power did not come as a surprise to Serena. Having worked hard to improve her tennis game, Serena had faith in her ability. Rallying regularly with Venus, now a professional, had convinced Serena that she could hold her own against other pros. By the time she was fourteen, Serena was eager to launch her own professional career. She wanted to join Venus and compete on the women's professional tour.

Another person who thought she was ready was Coach Macci. After watching the young teen play, he told a reporter for the Associated Press that Serena was on the verge of leaping up to the next level of competition. "In six months she'll be ready to rumble," Macci said.

As Venus had done earlier, Serena began bugging her parents to let her enter professional tournaments. Although shorter than Venus at 5 feet, 6 inches (she would eventually grow four more inches), the fourteen year old was incredibly strong and determined. Unlike her sister, Serena didn't have the long

Serena, between Richard and Venus, *was still in her sister's shadow in 1994 but would soon make her own professional debut.*

legs and long arms that would help her reach the ball quickly. So she used her court savvy to make up for her smaller size. By anticipating where her opponent would hit the ball, Serena could get in position to return a shot before it crossed the net. That split-second advantage allowed her to better control the return shot.

Confident in her skills and convinced she was ready to compete against the world's best female tennis players, Serena had to cross one more hurdle. Like Venus, she needed her parents' permission to play professionally. Eventually, Richard and Oracene reluctantly agreed to let their youngest daughter enter her first professional match in 1995.

Unlike Venus, who attracted lots of media attention at her pro debut, Serena quietly launched her career at an unknown tournament in Canada near the end of the year. She was quickly eliminated from the contest, losing her first match 6—1, 6—1. Nevertheless, she was eager to compete again. Richard, however, wanted her to concentrate on her schoolwork. Although disappointed, Serena had to wait an entire year before playing in another professional match.

While Serena was focusing on her education, her

studies included watching how Venus handled herself in tournaments. Venus had entered just three professional events in 1995. At both the Acura Classic and the Canadian Open, she lost in the opening round. Undaunted, she returned to Oakland in late October for her second Bank of the West Classic. There, Venus won her first two matches before losing in the third round.

These victories helped Venus reach another milestone. The Women's Tennis Association (WTA) ranks players based on their performance in tournaments, and Venus's two wins in Oakland landed her in the rankings for the first time. Although her ranking was 321, a far cry from the number-one spot Venus dreamed of reaching, it was a start.

Venus played in four professional tournaments in 1996. Then age sixteen, she struggled in competition. In three events, she was eliminated in the first round. Still, she stayed positive and tried to learn from her mistakes. Those lessons began to pay off during the Acura Classic, where Venus won her first two matches before falling to tennis legend Steffi Graf in the third round. Richard developed an unusual strategy for softening the sting of a loss for Venus. "Every time she loses I pay her $50," he said.

Venus plays hard in the 1996 State Farm Evert Cup.

"Venus says she has more $50 bills than she knows what to do with."

In 1997, when Serena returned to competition, she was ready. In Chicago, playing in only her fifth professional event, she defeated seventh-ranked Mary Pierce and fourth-ranked Monica Seles before being eliminated herself in the semifinal round. The outstanding performance vaulted Serena from number 304 to number 102 in the world rankings. While some players get nervous when they face top ranked professionals, Serena approached her matches with confidence. "I never really think I'm going to lose, so I don't get nervous really," she told reporters.

After getting off to a slow start, Venus also did well in 1997. Her first highlight came early in the year, when she graduated from high school. Eager to continue her education, Venus enrolled in classes at Palm Beach Community College near her home. She took her schoolbooks with her on the road and studied before and after her matches. Venus was scheduled to play in twelve tournaments that year, beginning with the Evert Cup, where she reached the quarterfinals. Her best performance of the year came in late summer at her first-ever U.S. Open, held just outside New York City.

Venus enjoyed her stay in New York, and she watched in awe as a special ceremony was held to dedicate the new Arthur Ashe Stadium, named after an African-American tennis superstar. The first black man to win the U.S. Open, Ashe had captured the title in 1968. He was also a champion for civil rights—working to open doors and break down barriers for blacks in the United States. Venus, who met Ashe in 1992, a year before he passed away, called him one of her heroes. "He was a great role model," Venus said. "Not just on the court, but off the court."

Perhaps inspired by Arthur Ashe, Venus was unstoppable on the court. She sailed through her first three matches to reach the quarterfinals, where she faced Sandrine Testud. Testud battled hard, but Venus took the first two sets to reach the semifinals of a professional tournament for the first time in her career. Next to go was Irina Spirlea of Romania, who also fought hard but ultimately fell in the wake of Venus's smoking serve.

Venus, then seventeen, faced another talented seventeen year old—Martina Hingis—in the final. Hingis quickly captured the first set, winning 6–0. Venus put up a better fight in the second set, but Hingis was more focused. The Swiss teen took the final set 6–4 to win the 1997 U.S. Open. Although disappointed, Venus was gracious in defeat. "You guys couldn't have a better winner for this tournament," she told reporters afterward.

Venus had lost that contest. But to tennis observers everywhere, it was clear that she was poised for greatness. And it was clear that her little sister wasn't far behind.

Richard proudly cheers on his two daughters with signs and smiles.

"Welcome to the Williams Show!!"

Female tennis professionals found themselves facing double trouble in 1998. That year, Serena earned her high school diploma and joined Venus at nearly a dozen tournaments.

The first stop for the Williams sisters was Sydney, Australia, where Serena wowed fans by winning her first three rounds in the Sydney International. She finally fell to Arantxa Sanchez-Vicario in the semifinals. Venus, who captured her first four rounds, faced Sanchez-Vicario in the finals. She, too, was overpowered by Sanchez-Vicario, losing 1—6, 3—6.

Venus and Serena made history at their next tournament, the Australian Open, one of the four grand slam events. After winning their opening rounds, the sisters faced one another for the first time in their professional careers. More than bragging rights were at stake, as the winner would advance to the quarterfinals. Both sisters played hard, with Venus prevailing 7—6, 6—1.

"It wasn't so funny, eliminating my little sister, but I have to be tough," Venus told reporters. "Since I've always been older, I had the feeling that I should win. After the match, I was like, 'Serena, I'm sorry to take you out. I really didn't want to, but I had to.'"

Venus, herself, lost in the following round, when Lindsay Davenport ousted her in three sets. Still, Venus came home with her first grand slam trophy. She teamed up with Justin Gimelstob to play mixed doubles (one male and one female player on a team). Dominating the final match, they defeated Cyril Suk and Helena Sukova, 6—2, 6—1, to win the 1998 Australian Open mixed doubles championship.

A few weeks later, Venus captured her first singles title at the IGA Tennis Classic in Oklahoma City.

Venus's height competed with Serena's speed in the 1998 Australian Open.

With a score of 6–3, 6–2, she knocked off South Africa's Joannette Kruger, who had defeated Serena in the quarterfinals. Venus continued her winning ways when she and Serena teamed up to play women's doubles. They captured the IGA doubles title before returning to their home in Florida.

In between tournaments, Venus and Serena took time to enjoy themselves. Playing video games, romping with their three dogs—Princess, Queen, and

Chase—talking about boys, and shopping helped them relax. Both enjoy listening to music, especially alternative rock songs. After years of playing air guitar on her tennis racket, Venus bought a real guitar and began learning how to play it. Serena started learning to play the drums. They enjoyed practicing together in the evenings.

Other favorite activities of the sisters included in-line skating, basketball, and tae kwon do. When the surf was up, Venus and Serena enjoyed riding the waves on brand-new surfboards. "I had a rotten, ugly, horrible, nasty, funky boogie board," Serena said. "I got a short board so I could rip and shred, but Venus went crazy and got a ten-footer."

Their fellow competitors probably wished the Williams sisters had kept on surfing instead of showing up at Key Biscayne, Florida, for the 1998 Lipton Championships in late March. There, Serena eliminated four competitors, including three top-ranked players, before losing in the quarterfinals to Martina Hingis. Venus proved too tough for Hingis in the semifinals and then went on to beat Anna Kournikova in the finals to earn her second career singles title.

Venus and Serena took some time off after the

Lipton Championships before jetting off to Europe in late spring. Their first stop was the Italian Open, played on clay courts. Both sisters breezed through the early rounds and met up against one another in the quarterfinals. For the second time that year, Venus defeated Serena, knocking her out of the tournament before being eliminated herself in the following round.

Seeing how stressful it was for Venus and Serena to compete against each other, Richard suggested that they play in separate events whenever possible. So Serena flew to Paris for the Open Gaz de France in February 1999, while Venus went to Oklahoma City to defend her IGA Classic title. The strategy worked. The Williams sisters both won titles in the same week. Although five thousand miles apart, the two kept in close contact between matches via e-mail. "When we were doing instant message on AOL I swear I could hear Venus laughing," Serena said.

Neither Serena nor Venus was laughing three weeks later when they faced each other in the finals of the Lipton Championships. Both of them were nervous and made numerous unforced errors. Venus regained her calm and prevailed, beating Serena 6–1, 4–6, 6–4. While they played, their father watched from the stands. He held a sign reading: "Welcome to the Williams Show!!"

The sisters walked off the court after the match with Venus's arm around Serena's shoulder. Serena took the loss calmly. "It doesn't affect how we feel about each other," she said. "Family comes first, no matter how many times we play each other."

Serena rebounded from the loss and began playing with much more confidence and control. She was on the top of her game in early August when she won the Acura Classic in Los Angeles. Soon

The Williams sisters remain close even as they become tennis rivals.

afterward, she electrified the sporting world when she charged through the quarterfinal and semifinal rounds to reach the finals of the U.S. Open. Spectators watched breathlessly as Serena took a commanding lead over Martina Hingis but then faltered in the second set. Then Serena dug deep, hanging onto a slim lead to upset Hingis in the tiebreaker. Serena was exultant as she accepted the U.S. Open trophy—the first grand slam trophy for one of the Williams sisters.

Tennis experts had predicted for years that the Williams sisters would be grand slam champions. Venus was older, with more professional experience, and many people expected her to be the first sister to take top honors. But Serena surprised everyone with her exciting U.S. Open win. Still red-hot a month later, Serena faced Venus again in the finals of the Grand Slam Cup in Germany. This time, Serena was the Williams with the advantage, defeating Venus 6–1, 3–6, 6–3.

For years she had played in her big sister's shadow. But 1999 had become Serena's time to shine.

Richard poses in front of Serena and Venus's new tournament bus.

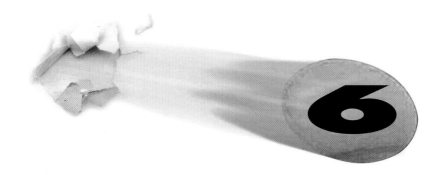

Sisters on Top

For years, Venus and Serena Williams had boldly proclaimed they would someday dominate women's professional tennis. By 2000, that day had clearly arrived. They began the year listed at number three (Venus) and number four (Serena) in the women's professional rankings. They were both confident and playing strong, powerful tennis. Eager for a chance to improve their rankings, they looked forward to competing. But pain in her wrists forced Venus to withdraw from the Australian Open. Her doctor told her that she had a condition called tendonitis, caused by playing too much tennis. Venus was advised to rest her wrists and stay off the court.

The layoff gave her more time to focus on her schoolwork. At Palm Beach Community College, she studied fashion design and fell in love with her courses. Always a serious student, Venus had long told her family that she wanted to be a fashion designer or an architect after she stopped playing tennis professionally.

While Venus remained in Florida to heal from her injuries, Serena headed to Europe. There she played well, making it to the finals in the Open Gaz de France and winning the Faber Grand Prix in Germany. Then she too took some time off. Injuring her knee in April, she returned to Florida for treatment. Like Venus, she kept busy while off the court. The two sisters bought a house down the street from their parents' home. They enjoyed shopping for furnishings for their new digs.

Venus's wrists recovered in time for the French Open. Looking rusty, she used the tournament to tune up for the All-England Lawn Tennis Championships— better known as Wimbledon—just outside London. A healthy Serena planned to join her for the world-famous event. The Williams sisters showed up in England with a new look. Their colorful beads were gone, and their long, flowing braids were pulled back with decorated bands. The new look got a lot of attention, as both Venus and Serena took center stage at the grand slam event. Confident they would outshine the competition, both sisters had even bought gowns to wear at the Winner's Ball before leaving Florida.

Both Venus and Serena backed their confidence with strong play in the early rounds. Serena dominated Lisa Raymond in the quarterfinals, taking just forty-one minutes to win the match. Venus, who faced Martina Hingis in her quarterfinal round, had a

Serena stays focused during the first round of Wimbledon 2000.

much tougher time. She pressed through for a 6—3, 4—6, 6—4 victory to set up her fifth professional match with Serena.

Tennis fans were fascinated by the idea of two sisters facing one another at one of the world's most famous tennis tournaments. But for all the buildup, the semifinal meeting was a letdown. Neither player found her rhythm in the match, and play was lackluster from both sides of the court. Venus made

Wimbledon's crowds could not wait to see sister against sister, although it was difficult for Venus and Serena to play each other.

fewer errors and eventually took charge of the match, winning 6–2, 7–6. Serena fought back tears as the two met at the net after the match. Venus put her arm around Serena's shoulder and led her off court.

Later, Venus noted how hard it was to defeat her sister. "I felt sad because I'm the big sister and I'm supposed to take care of her," Venus said. "It's really bitter, but someone had to move on. Serena is a real competitor, even more than I am, so this really hurts her deep."

Both Venus and Serena were much happier when Venus faced Lindsay Davenport in the event final. Davenport had won the Wimbledon trophy the year before. This year, however, Venus overpowered her, taking the match 6–3, 7–6. When the match was over, a joyous Venus leaped into the air. Her arms outstretched with happiness, she beamed in triumph. The Williams sisters added another grand slam trophy to their collection before leaving London. Two days after Venus's singles win, they beat Julie Halard-Decugis and Ai Sugiyma, 6–3, 6–1, in the women's doubles final.

Venus proved her Wimbledon victory wasn't a fluke by winning her next two tournaments. Riding a twenty-match win streak going into the U.S. Open, she was determined to keep her run going. Her determination paid off in the semifinals, where she faced top-ranked Martina Hingis. In the decisive third set, with Hingis just two points from victory, Venus made a comeback. Rallying strongly, she overcame a third set deficit and took the match 4–6, 6–3, 7–5. Facing Lindsay Davenport, who had eliminated Serena in the quarterfinals, Venus captured the 2000 U.S. Open title with a 6–4, 7–5 win. Serena, who had won the title in 1999, ran down to the court after the match to congratulate her sister.

The following week, while engravers were inscribing Venus's name on the silver championship trophy next to Serena's name from the year before, the two were busy packing their bags. Venus and Serena had been chosen to play on the United States doubles tennis team at the 2000 Olympics. Venus would play in the Olympic singles tournament. They flew to Sydney, Australia, shortly after the U.S. Open ended.

At the Games, Venus ran her incredible win streak to thirty-two matches, including a 6–2, 6–4 victory over Russia's Elena Dementieva for the women's singles gold medal. She captured her second gold medal the following day when she teamed up with Serena in

Center court is packed with Williams fans at the 2000 Summer Olympics in Sydney, Australia.

the doubles final. The Williamses crushed Kristie Boogert and Miriam Oremans of the Netherlands, 6—1, 6—1, to become Olympic champions.

After the doubles win, Venus summed up her feelings about being part of what is surely the greatest sister team in sports history. "For me, this is almost bigger than singles," Venus said. "It's right up there because I have this victory with Serena, my sister, family member, my best friend."

For these tennis sensations, sharing the spotlight with a sister is the ultimate victory.

Career Highlights

Venus's Career Highlights

2000
- won singles titles at Wimbledon, Bank of the West Classic, Acura Tennis Classic, Pilot Pen International, U.S. Open
- won gold medal at the Olympic Games in Sydney, Australia
- ended the year ranked number 3 on the WTA Tour

1999
- won singles titles at IGA Tennis Classic, Lipton Championships, Betty Barclay Cup, Italian Open, Pilot Pen International, Swisscom Challenge
- named to the Fed Cup team
- ended the year ranked number 3

1998
- won singles titles at IGA Tennis Classic, Lipton Championships, Grand Slam Cup
- clocked a women's world record 127-mph serve at the Swisscom Challenge
- won mixed doubles titles with Justin Gimelstob at Australian Open and French Open
- ended the year ranked number 5

1997
- reached finals at U.S. Open, first woman to reach finals in her Open debut since 1978
- ended the year ranked number 99

Serena's Career Highlights

2000
- won singles titles at Faber Grand Prix, Los Angeles Open, Princess Cup, Grand Slam Cup
- ended the year ranked number 6 on the WTA Tour

1999
- won singles titles at Paris Indoors, Evert Cup, Acura Classic, U.S. Open, Grand Slam Cup
- named to the Fed Cup team
- ended the year ranked number 4

1998
- won mixed doubles titles with Max Mirnyi at U.S. Open and Wimbledon
- ended the year ranked number 20

1997
- entered the WTA Tour world rankings at number 453, three weeks later ranked number 102

Venus and Serena's Doubles Play Highlights

2000
- won gold medal at the Olympic Games in Sydney, Australia
- won doubles title at Wimbledon

1999
- won doubles titles at French Open, U.S. Open, Faber Grand Prix

1998
- won doubles titles at IGA Tennis Classic, Swisscom Challenge

Glossary

center court: The central court at a tennis center, usually the site of the most important matches at tournaments.

doubles tennis: Tennis competition with two players on a team. Women's doubles teams have two female players, and mixed doubles teams have one male and one female player.

elimination tournament: A tennis tournament in which only players who win their games can advance to the next round of play.

set: A portion of a tennis match consisting of a series of games. The first player to win six games, with a lead of at least two games, wins the set.

tiebreaker: A play-off game in tennis, used to determine a winner when a set is tied six games to six. The first player to score seven points, with a lead of at least two points, wins the tiebreaker.

unforced error: A lost point caused by a player's mistake, such as hitting the ball into the net or hitting it out of bounds.

Sources

The information in this book came from the following sources: Virginia Aronson (*Venus Williams,* Chelsea House, 1999); Associated Press, 28 February 1999, 27 March 1999, 30 March 1999, 3 October 1999, 4 October 1999, 7 July 2000, 9 July 2000, 10 July 2000; *Business Week,* 29 September 1997; *Ebony,* May 1995; Robin Finn (*New York Times,* 12 September 1999); David Higdon (*Tennis* magazine article on www.williamsisters.com); Bruce Jenkins (*San Francisco Chronicle,* 6 September 1999, 10 July 2000); Pat Jordan (*New York Times Magazine,* 16 March 1997); msnbc.com (8 July 2000); Fred Mullane (www.justwomen.com); Michael Neal (*People,* 27 October 1997, 29 December 1997); Marc Peyser and Allison Samuels (*Newsweek,* 24 August 1998); S. L. Price (*Sports Illustrated,* 20 September 1999); *San Jose Mercury News,* 30 July 1999, 31 July 1999, 2 August 1999, 16 August 1999, 29 August 1999, 10 September 1999, 11 September 1999, 12 September 1999, 13 September 1999, 17 September 1999, 2 October 1999, 4 June 2000, 5 June 2000, 5 July 2000, 6 July 2000, 7 July 2000, 9 July 2000, 27 July 2000, 27 August 2000, 29 August 2000, 6 September 2000, 7 September 2000; Bruce Schoenfeld (*Tennis Match* article on www.williamssisters.com); *Seventeen,* 16 April 1996; *Sports Illustrated,* 15 September 1997; Sonja Steptoe (*Sports Illustrated,* 10 June 1991); Michael Teitelbaum (*Venus Williams: Grand Slam Star,* HarperActive, 1998); Steve Wilstein (Associated Press, 31 August 1999, 7 September 1999, 9 September 1999, 4 June 2000); www.williamssisters.com.

Index

Write to Venus and Serena:

You can send mail to Venus and Serena at the address on the right. If you write a letter, don't get your hopes up too high. Venus, Serena, and other athletes get lots of letters every day, and they aren't always able to answer them all.

Venus and Serena Williams
c/o WTA TOUR
1266 East Main Street,
Floor 4
Stamford, CT 06902

Acknowledgments

Photographs reproduced with permission of: ©ALLSPORT USA/Gary M. Prior, pp. 1, 47; ©ALLSPORT USA/Clive Brunskill, pp. 2, 55, 56, 59; SportsChrome East/West, Bongarts Photography, Peter Schatz, p. 6; SportsChrome East/West, Rob Tringali Jr., pp. 11, 13; Sports-Chrome East/West, Bongarts Photography, Mark Sandten, p. 15; ©ALLSPORT USA/Ken Levine, pp. 16, 22, 23, 24, 27, 29; ©Reuters New Media Inc./CORBIS, p. 35; ©ALLSPORT USA/Al Bello, pp. 32, 38, 44, 50; ©ALLSPORT USA/Jamie Squire, p. 41; ©Chuck Solomon/SI/Icon SMI, p. 52.
Front cover photographs by ©Carol L. Newsom (right), ©ALLSPORT USA/Clive Brunskill (left), SportsChrome East/West, ©Bongarts (background).
Back cover photographs by ©ALLSPORT USA/Clive Brunskill (both).

About the Author

Terri Morgan is a freelance writer and sports fan from Soquel, California. Her articles have appeared in over four dozen magazines and newspapers. Her other books for Lerner include: *Photography: Take Your Best Shot, Steve Young: Complete Quarterback* (both with Shmuel Thaler), *Ruthie Bolton-Holifield: Sharpshooting Playmaker*, and *Gabrielle Reece: Volleyball's Model Athlete*. When not writing, Terri enjoys surfing, walking her dogs, playing baseball, and watching sports.